JB24

MW01528862

Printed in the United States of America

First Printing, 2016

ASIN: B019DFM395

Laugh With Nikita B Publishing
A division of Nikita B Unlimited, LLC
P.O. Box 37054
Rock Hill, SC 29732

www.nikitabwilliams.com

WHAT DO OTHERS THINK ABOUT NIKITA B? (I'm glad you asked)

As a former talent educator, one of the things I love most is to see someone using their intellect & gifts to their fullest potential. Nikita has an amazing ability to carefully listen & then quickly synthesize someone's words into a thorough analysis while at the same time offering sound advice/guidance. So not only is she a healer of people's spirits through laughter, she is gifted with the ability to lead & enlighten in a way few are able. Yet I sense a lovely sensitivity and thoughtfulness within her as well that allows her to "tune into" people & quickly analyze what's needed. I share all of this to say that I see Nikita as nothing less than, FIERCELY AMAZING! *Anna DeBose Hankins, Talent Strategist, Columbia Maryland*

DEDICATIONS

This book is dedicated to ALL of my family, friends and supporters. I want each of you to know that I LOVE YOU TO LIFE. There is nothing that you can't accomplish once you conquer fear. Just as you all go through different levels of fear, so do I. But, I want you to hear my heart when I say YOU CAN DO IT! To the people who are always putting everyone else before them and not truly living a life of fulfillment; I dedicate this to YOU. Remember if you can see it in your mind then you can hold it in your hand. I believe in YOU, I LOVE YOU and I'm cheering for YOU! From your #HopeDealer and #PurposePusher!

IN MEMORY OF

This book is in memory of my beautiful mother Veronica Kirk Blakeney; a woman that lived a fearless life and taught me to do the same. She never focused on what we didn't have and always used what we had to her fullest capability. She never let the opinions of others become her truth. She was vivacious, triumphant, tenacious as well as a bold woman of God. She lived her life to the fullest even as she battled triple negative breast cancer. The lord answered her prayers and granted her a sweet hour in June, 2010 when she transitioned to be.

This is also in memory of my baby brother Ronnie Blakeney, Jr "aka" (Shot Dogg.) If only you would have met this guy. He was a perfect example of designing your own life and living it out loud. He was hilarious, spontaneous and a firm believer of living your dreams. He was loved by both the young and old, he was a force to be reckoned with and his legacy still lives on today through his daughter. My mother left me with so much wisdom and compassion for others that it ignited a burning desire in me to push past my fears and live a life that I love. Since I made that decision I designed the life that I desired to live and I have been living it ever since.

BECAUSE OF YOU I WILL ALWAYS SHOW UP AT MY BEST, EXPOSE THE BEST IN OTHERS AND WILL NEVER SETTLE FOR GOOD WHEN BETTER IS AVAILABLE! I LOVE YOU BOTH BEYOND MEASURE.

Until We Meet Again! "Skeedah"

TABLE OF CONTENTS

FOREWARD

When a person decides to tenaciously devote their time and talent to write from the war room of their own personal struggles and battles with fear, you must stop everything that you are doing in life and read it.

Fear has no prejudices and very few people escape through life without first having to face their biggest fears head on. "Beating the F out of Fear" by Comedian Nikita B Williams forces you to dance in the dark with your Fears while your Faith is tested and tried.

Through a series of personal reflections, Nikita borrows moments of pain and extreme fear in exchange for a playbook strategically written for fighters who desire to win in life.

Beating the F Out of Fear will require you to "Faith It" until you "Make It," you will begin to see yourself the way that God sees you. Your life will have to change because there is simply, No Failure in God. "We have all been given the "gift of life" but we are not all a "gift to life" If you are reading this right now, you have been given the gift of life.

The Billion Dollar Question is Why?
I believe there comes a time in everyone's life where you must question the purpose of your very own existence. What are you supposed to be doing and what is stopping you from accomplishing it? Who are you supposed to be serving and what roadblocks have you avoided because you were too afraid of what was ahead? Why are you alive at this specific time in history? What will you offer this earth? What will you leave behind for others to experience? Will this earth know that you were here?

I, like Nikita and probably like many of you reading this book, have or will experience your fair share of broken dreams, promises, loss, betrayal, lack, stagnation, confusion, disappointments, and fear. I believe Fear in and of itself isn't all bad, in fact fear serves an incredibly important purpose. Fear alerts the human body that something is wrong. It's called the fight or flight response. In the moments that we experience extreme fear, we have a choice to stay and fight or take flight to safer grounds. When we experience fear without making a choice its called anxiety and anxiety left unchecked may lead to debilitating depression, and depression left unchecked may lead to death. Not a physical death, but the death of your dreams, your goals, your future, your marriage, your business, and your personal happiness.

Words have incredible power over how your mind responds to your innate gifts and callings. What you speak with your mouth becomes what you believe in your heart, and what you believe in your heart somehow determines the trajectory of your future.

Once you realize the power you have over fear, you will begin to win the war of life.
I believe with all my heart that every human being born of a woman has a purpose tailor-made for their life it is vested in our DNA.

Nikita B. Williams calls herself a hope dealer and a purpose pusher, but I see her more as a Strategic Life-Midwife who forces you to deliver your baby. It is not enough to live in your dreams alone and Nikita B Williams explains this in this easy to read yet profound book. While having a dream might impregnate you with desire, if you fail to deliver your baby, you will never be able to eat from the fruit of your own labor. You will forever be forced to sow into other dreamers: dreams, while you, yourself, settle for a life paralyzed with fear.

I challenge you to read this book with an impregnated mind anxiously waiting for your water to break so that you might give birth to your Faith and abort the destructive cycles of fears that have been holding you back for so long. Reap the rewards of self-discovery, unashamedly & fearless. Do your part to protect, invest, and seek out your higher calling in life. Become the gift.

Portia Chandler ~an unwrapped gift

PREFACE

I wrote this book with you in mind because I knew how it felt to be afraid to do the things that I really desired and aspired to do. I can remember the void that I felt every time an opportunity passed me by that I knew I was capable of doing. The purpose of this book is to identify your fear factors and show you a way out. As I was writing this book I reminisced on all the times that I experienced fear and how much time I wasted focusing on the "what IF's" only for the "IF" to never happened. In this book you will identify with the fear factors that most of us face. But, it doesn't stop there. You will also be given a solution as to how you can face and conquer the fear and start living a life that you love.

ACKNOWLEDGEMENT

I'd like to first and foremost acknowledge God for being who he is in my life and loving me beyond my faults. I want to also acknowledge my family; Husband, Tarrance, Children; Hykeim, DayQwann, Alexandria, Kerya, J'Quida and Byron (wheeeew-weee....lol) I'd also like to acknowledge my father, Pastor Ronnie E. Blakeney, Sr, My siblings; sister, Angela and brother EdRico. I also want to acknowledge both my Blakeney and Kirk family (too many names to mention) but, I'd be remised not to speak the names of both of my beautiful grandmothers Ms. Shirley Miller and Ella Mae Kirk in which I'm blessed to still have in my life. These ladies are the pillar to our families and were also great examples of how to live a fearless life. I want to thank you all for always being in my corner and encouraging me to keep going and not give up. For the shows you attended, the encouraging words you gave, the inspiration you give me when I visit and for the experiences that we shared in my youth that I've made the premise to my material that I've shared on stages around the world. I thank you all in advance for making me famous (smile.)

INTRODUCTION

In life you may have tried many things. I'm sure you may have attempted things that you knew wasn't right for you and I'm also sure that you have attempted things that you really wanted to accomplish and may have failed at them both. Think about it there were times that you have not only thought that you would fail, but you expected to fail when it came to doing something new. Even though failure was a constant factor in your life you didn't allow it to be an end all for you. I can't remember a time that I was successful the first go round. Although this was the pattern of the way things went for me so was my tenacity and fortitude to "make things happen."

No matter how hard I fell I made it a point to get back up. My head was harder than a brick wall and whatever you told me not to do; if I wanted to do it I did it anyway. In spite of the obstacles, barriers and defeats I found a way to make things happen no matter what. Can you relate to any of this? I'm sure this didn't come easy for you, but it comes natural. There was always something within me that would push me to keep going.

There may be many times that you have to talk to yourself and shake things off in order to stay focused. I was usually the "go to" person for advice, assistance, guidance and support. The downside to that was it was very seldom that I ever had someone to go to when I needed it. I started to be in a place in my life that I had never been before. I took the disadvantages of my failures and used them to my advantage. I learned from my mistakes and I kept pressing. Through the abusive relationships, misfortunes, unexpected death of my brother, untimely death of my mother, being betrayed by close family and friends, losing everything to a house fire and having to start over; I'd say I had many opportunities to walk away from it all.

I was finally in a place in my life where I was elevating above the status quo, I was no longer on public assistance and I no longer felt like I had to settle for less than what I wanted. But now the "inner hater" had arrived. The same voice that use to tell me "get yourself together and to make things happen and keep it moving" had now turned against me. I started reflecting on all the past failures versus my wins. I looked at the friends and family that I no longer had around me instead of the ones who were still there cheering me on. Here I was in a better place than I had ever been before and found it to be more difficult to pull myself up and get things together when it came to me moving forward.

I found myself "stuck" in a place that I didn't want to be in and had no clue as to how I would get out of it. To everyone else I had "arrived" but deep inside I felt like I couldn't move. Fear had found its way in my mind and infected my desires, aspirations and ambitions with doubt, limited beliefs and a lack of confidence. Although I went from public assistance to public success there was still enough room for fear to play tricks with me and try to rearrange my thought process. Not only was I now running a high risk of returning back to a place in my life that I promised myself that I would never return to but I was also on the verge of losing everything that I had worked so hard to achieve. It was then I decided that the strength and effort that I would have to use to throw it all away; I'd use that same strength and effort to "Beat the F out Of Fear" AND LAUNCH MY DREAMS!

Let's Get It Started!

CHAPTER ONE

THE FEAR OF THE UNKNOWN

When I first told my family and friends that I was going to write a book they were ecstatic. But when I told them the title of the book they were "what, why, oh my goodness, huh?" The first thing that I thought about was the song writer Betty Wright when she played the song "Tonight Is the Night" for her mom. It was a song about a young girl losing her virginity. Her mom listened to the song and said "I like the music, the melody it sounds really nice, but I know you're not going to sing that song." This song ended up being one of her biggest hits and hit the top of the charts and is still one of the most played singles on old school radio today. Although Betty was afraid to take the song to her mom she knew her message would reach the masses and that many people would be able to relate. Had she not decided to face her fears, write what was on her heart and deliver it to the world we may have never known her and all of her greatness.

The title of my book had me feeling the same way. I knew that it may be controversial, but at the same time I also knew that it was a message meant for the masses. I knew that the things that I had written about my experiences with fear and how I conquered it would be someone else's breakthrough. When you take the "F" out of fear, or "beat the "F" out of it as I like to say you're left with the word "ear." We use our ears as channels to listen and hear the things that are going on around us as well as hear those who are communicating with us. Because hearing and listening is so important we were giving a channel on each side so that we are aware of all things around us. More importantly, we have to remember that the things that we hear and listen to have such an impact on us that if we listen to them long enough we will begin to believe them. My life has been full of unexpected challenges that caused me to use fear as an excuse for not pursuing my goals. I went through years of abuse and hearing how I would never accomplish anything and how nobody would have be interested in me or want me to be a part of their life. Even though my family always lifted me up it was the words of my abuser that rang in my ear every time I desired to do something different. Although I was encouraged to be great all of my childhood, my adulthood consist of episodes, circumstances and situations that spoke the opposite.

I struggled with low self –esteem, depression, low self-worth and no confidence. The words that I heard as an adult weighed so much heavier than those of my childhood that I had allowed myself to believe. No longer did I believe I could be whoever I wanted to be or do whatever I wanted to do or have what I wanted to have. I had allowed the negative words of toxic people to invade my belief system. It was then that I realized that what you listen to leads you. The things I knew that I could do and the person that I knew I was I no longer believed in. After many years of upsets, setbacks and failures; I was finally able to find the confidence to separate myself from the toxic people in my life. I was bolder in ways that I had never been before. I set boundaries for myself and finally I believed in my abilities again. Since then I have been able to build my dreams and experience joy in every area of my life. I want to show you how to beat the "F" out of fear just as I have. Not only is it time to beat the "F" out of fear, but it's also time to replace it with faith. I know this is easier said than done, but I'm here to show you how to "faith it until you make it."

When I ask people why they aren't living their dreams or pursuing their goals and aspirations they usually give me an answer out of the "fierce 4" which is either the fear of the unknown, the fear of failure, the fear of success or the fear of doing it alone. As we all know fear will paralyze you from growth in your life both personally as well as in business. Imagine going into a dark room that you've never been in before. Even though you may know that there is nothing in the room that can harm you the fact that you can't actually see it sends a sense of fear to raise in you because you truly don't know what's there. Well life is the same way. When we don't know the answers we tend to create scenarios that we think may happen and then base our decisions on the illusion that we created as if it's real. We fear that because we don't know what to do there's no need to do anything. We don't know if we'll be accepted so to avoid being rejected we don't move forward. We don't have all the answers and we're afraid to ask the questions. Even when we feel like we may be on to something if we don't know what's next and don't know who to seek to find the answers we fall right back in a place of complacency and do nothing.

Not having answers to our problems can definitely hider us from growing in the way that we desire to grow. But, being afraid to find he answers is the death of success. Have you ever felt as if your best wasn't good enough? You're exhausted from trying to make sure that everyone around you has their needs met. Let me guess you're the spouse, the child, the parent, the sibling or maybe even the close friend of people that really need you. I mean if you weren't there to help them what would they do? You're assisting everyone but yourself in being fulfilled and accomplishing things meanwhile you sit in a place of emptiness and walk around with a constant void and the "what about me" complex. You may have even had so many challenges in your life that you feel like you can't possibly be the person you want to be or do the things that you have desired to do in life. Many of us know exactly how we ended up where we are, but have no idea as to how to become "unstuck" and move forward from that dark place.

There are so many factors that can and will play a part in our thinking and thought process. Just think about it; when you were a child you had an imagination that developed the most peaceful places for you to reside. You believed that you could conquer the world and nothing could stand in your way. But then life happens. You begin to encounter different things and different people. You hear the opinions of others and what they think about you and you begin to process their comments as your truths. So now instead of believing as you did as a kid, you have now developed a complex that you have carried into your adulthood. You may have been told you're too big, too small, too short or too tall. Some may say you're too dark, you're too pale or for my bi-racial family you may have been rejected simply because you were blessed enough to share the ethnicity of more than one person or culture. You have allowed things that are a part of you that others see as issues hinder you from moving forward.

It's time that you use the power of imagination again. Imagine that you're not in the situation that you're currently in. What does that look like for you? You have to remember that it's impossible to have a dream for yourself without first having an imagination. Before any great invention or big success was accomplished the inventor or successor had to first imagine that things were already accomplished. You have so much power within yourself that it's truly unexplainable. If only you would believe your life would change in ways that you wouldn't think was possible, then and only then will you be motivated to take fear and jump with it. Because fear of the "unknown" is based on myths, mystery as well as a bunch of "ifs" you can't really address or pin point the issue. Truth of the matter is you will be more stressed and go through more pain being afraid of doing something than you will from actually doing what you're fearing. The best way to conquer the fear of the unknown is by mindset mastery. You must understand that there is favor in focus. Whenever you focus on what you want to accomplish and use what you already have available to you it leaves less room for you to be anxious and excitable about things that may or may not happen. It's important that you become single-minded. In this book that I love to read it tells us that a double minded man is unstable in all of his ways. You must first get clear about what you want to accomplish. Often times the fear of the unknown comes about because we're unclear as to what we really want to accomplish. When we lack clarity we become overwhelmed and we become overwhelmed we lack direction, thus enhancing our fear of the unknown. So if you want to beat the fear of the unknown you must first know what you want to accomplish.

Write down your TOP 5 "What If's" and then write the complete opposite (positive) response on the other side of it. When these thoughts come back to mind, IMMEDIATELY replace them with a positive response.

Example:

What if I try and I don't know what to do?

(RESPONSE) I have EVERYTHING that I need to get started!

1)

Response:

2)

Response:

3)

Response:

4)

Response:

5)

Response:

CHAPTER TWO

THE FEAR OF FAILURE

Fear will keep you from applying for a certain job, starting a business, having a difficult conversation, taking a chance or trying something new. Over the years, I've talked about fear and the power it can have in holding you back. But fear can also be an indicator. It's an indicator that you want something more...something different...something better. Rarely do you experience fear when we are in our comfort zone. It's only when you start thinking about making a change – a shift – that could move you closer to your vision and your goals that fear rise up in you. Have you ever wanted to do something so badly you could almost taste it?

I mean you knew that this thing was for you, but now that it's time for you to take yourself seriously you find yourself afraid to take the leap because you're afraid of failing. If you try and fail you may have to live through the embarrassment of facing the ones that told you it was a bad idea and tried to detour you from doing it. Failing could be a great experience for you and you could learn valuable lessons from it. But, be honest with yourself, who really wants to fail? My dad always told me that the enemy comes to kill, steal and destroy so I had to have something promising within me because if I didn't he wouldn't bother me.

The fear of failure is one of the hardest fears to conquer simply because you have to convince yourself that you are good enough with what you already have. Often times when you fear failing at something it's because you feel the need to be validated when the truth of the matter is there are no additives needed you are already more than enough. When someone thinks that they have to become certified in something that they are gifted at and already do they sometimes feel like the certification is a way to say "yes I can do this, see look at what I have." But, you must know that a certification or degree isn't worth the paper that it's written on if you're afraid to use it.

Before you can change your life or make improvements you have to first decide what it is that you want to change and what improvements you want to make. Writing your goals out is the first step to success – the mere process of writing down your goals allows you to see first-hand what is a priority. Your mind focuses on it – you're telling your mind "this is a priority – let's focus on it." Your subconscious mind then picks up this message and looks at it as a priority. But if you simply write down your goals and not do anything about it – nothing will change. By making it a priority – you get your mind and subconscious mind working for you. I know there are some of you who may say: I can't think of any goals – I don't have any goals but I know I just want things to get better." Without goals you have no direction – without direction you can never get anywhere because you don't know where you're going.

You need direction to go the distance and a confused mind does absolutely nothing. If you want things to get better – then you really do have goals – you just haven't thought about them enough. If this is where you are then decide how things would get better – what would life be like if things were to get better? What does "better" mean? Think ahead to 5 years from now – if you had the ideal life – what would it be like? As you think about this you'll start to come up with your list of goals. Get your mind and subconscious mind to focus on the specifics and you'll get results. Stay with vague goals and you'll get vague results. So every day you need to think about your goals and think about what you can do to achieve them – you need to stick to the plan. If your goals are a priority then you need to keep them on your mind. Too often people list their goals and then forget about them. At the end of the year or at the start of a new year they list the same goals and they forget about them again. They never think about them and they never try to find ways to achieve them. They let their mind focus on whatever it chooses, they get caught up in the routines of everyday life and they forget about their priorities. Most people lose focus of their goals because they don't have a plan. Here's where change begins – by focusing on your goals and having a plan. When I say focus I just want you to think about your goals, think about why they are important, think about how much better life would be if you achieved them, then start thinking about what you can do to achieve them – create a plan and stick to it – go one step at a time.

Your reality is a direct reflection of your current thoughts. What is happening in your life – reflects what is going on in your mind and subconscious mind. Align your thoughts and beliefs with what you want to accomplish – and you will achieve your goals. The negative thoughts probably represent some of your beliefs – by doing this exercise you get a pretty good idea of the kind of work you're going to have to do in order to achieve your goals. Right now you need to be aware of what you need to change – because once you're aware you can then make a commitment to changing. If you had any positive thoughts about achieving those goals – then you need to continue focusing on those positive thoughts.

In the words of my drunk uncle and I quote "If you scared, go to church."

Now what does that mean exactly? I have no earthly idea, but you'd be amazed at how well it fits in a conversation when you're trying to push people to move forward………lol. Mind you this is the same uncle that tells all of his friends that he has a rich niece because he saw me on the internet. He was so excited about my accomplishments and wanted everybody to know that I was his "famous" niece. He said "she is famous, because she is *GOOGALABLE*!" This was hilarious to me. But then I thought about it, I am "GOOGALABLE." If you put my name in the search engine information and photos of me will appear. I've been on hundreds of stages, featured on television, interviewed on nationally syndicated radio shows as well as by many media personalities and I did it all scared. None of this would have been possible had I not taken fear and jumped with it. Because I was afraid of failing I prepared myself to win.

I didn't want to fail at comedy so I was mentored by some awesome comics. I wanted an undeniable brand so I invested in a phenomenal branding and business strategist. I wanted to be successful in both my personal life as well as business so I made sure I separated myself from toxic people. So because I was afraid to fail I equipped myself to be successful even if I failed. The great thing about being prepared to receive success is that even when you stumble and fall at times because you are aware of the process and have knowledgeable people around you, you'll have the tools and insight that you need to move forward as you work through the issues that may be faced with. If you desire to reach success you must get the information you need. Whether this is going through classes, seminars, coaching programs, mentorships, listening to audios or watching videos you use whatever method that suits you best. Then you must always have some sort of inspiration around you. Music inspires me; comedy inspires me as well as a great motivational speech. You have to find the things that inspire you and when you feel challenged or frustrated use one of your methods of inspiration to lift your spirit and boost your momentum. Lastly, you have to have implementation. It doesn't matter how great you are and what you have to offer if you're not doing anything with it. Through self-investment, information and inspiration I was able to fail my way to success and if you give yourself a chance and don't give up you can do the same.

To kick the fear of failure you must invest in yourself in one or most of the following ways:

READING and INFORMATION

EDUCATING YOURSELF ABOUT WHAT IT IS THAT YOU DESIRE TO ACHIEVE

MENTORSHIP

INSPIRATION

HIRING A COACH

HIRING YOUR WEAKNESS

GETTING AN ACCOUNTABILITY PARTNER

JOINING A SUPPORT GROUP OF LIKE MINDED INDIVIDUALS

CHAPTER THREE

THE FEAR OF SUCCESS

When you can clearly see how accomplishing your goals will change your life, your family, your fulfillment, your happiness, your finances, your community, or the world, it becomes unbearable not to act on it. It becomes painful to do nothing. You have to know exactly what you'll get, have, accomplish or receive IF you move past fear. That's why you have to a vision board – you have to see what you truly want every day as a reminder that you must face your fear or be willing to live without your vision. Having a vision isn't enough. What are the goals that you need to work on to get that vision. What actual steps do you need to take and how do you get there. What do you need to KNOW or LEARN? Knowledge diminishes fear AND builds confidence.

Usually when I say that people are afraid of succeeding I have people say "I'm not afraid to be successful that's that I want." But, do you really mean that? What happens when you're successful and then don't know how to keep up the momentum? When you get to a level that you've never been to before fear rises and tries to detour you from staying where you are. This is when you have the "Minnie hater" in your head trying to convince you that where you are isn't that bad. Success is an awesome place to be in, but it can be scary when you're afraid to do what it takes to keep up the momentum. Many of us think that if we achieve a certain level of success then we'll be happy. But, truth of the matter is having happiness in your life before you achieve success is the energy that you'll need to reach your goals.

Now when you think of your goals – start thinking about why they are important to you and then think about how you can achieve them. At first you may not have any answers when it comes to thinking about how you can achieve your goals – but as you do this more regularly your mind will seek out answers and your subconscious mind will guide you to those answers. By focusing on why these goals are important you get your mind to move in a new direction. It no longer thinks about why you can't achieve your goals – instead it's busy thinking about why you need to achieve them – and this spurs the mind and subconscious mind into action. Having a new thought habit is important because your thoughts create your beliefs and your beliefs create your reality. Your current pattern of thinking isn't working for you – and that's what you need to change. The art of discipline and success Have you ever met a successful person who was not disciplined?

Take a look at some of the most successful people – those that you feel are successful and you'll find that they are all disciplined individuals. They are disciplined in their work habits, personal habits, relationships and business or career. More importantly they all have money – or at least make a comfortable living. If you want to have more money you have to be disciplined enough to manage it well and take care of it. You have to know when to spend your money, on what and you have to be able to save. If you cannot save your money then you have no discipline and if you're not disciplined with your money – then there's no reason for you to have it – you simply can't take care of it. Therefore you will not attract situations to create more or save money – instead you will attract opportunities for you to spend your money.

By being disciplined in one area you'll find it easier to be disciplined in other areas – and thus you start to gain control of your mind, you start to direct your subconscious mind to create the life you want and you start regaining control of your life. Without discipline – you simply have chaos and disorder. Take a look around – if you have chaos and disorder then you need to start getting disciplined – one area at a time. If you're overweight and feel you can't control your eating habits it's because there is a lack of discipline – you're not in control – and once you start being more disciplined you'll regain control.

Keeping Your Commitment By listing your goals, analyzing your thoughts and creating new disciplines that will propel you to success you've basically made a commitment to achieve your goals. Now you need to keep that commitment and this is where most people fail. The reason they fail and the reason they break their commitment is because they forget their Top Priority and they forget why their goals are important. It's easy to slip back into old habits. The only way things are going to change is to create new habits. By doing this you'll begin eliminating the negative patterns that have limited you and created the situations that you don't want.

Right now you've got a good idea of what you want, what you need to do and what needs to be changed Consider everything an opportunity – when you put out a message – when you instruct your subconscious mind to find a solution or when you tell your subconscious mind that you have a Top Priority that needs to be achieved – it will make things happen. And when you're enjoying life – your subconscious mind creates more situations for you to enjoy life. When you focus on what you want – you'll begin to attract opportunities to make it happen and you'll get back on track and start following your calling. Finally – remember nothing happens overnight. I get a lot of people who want to create changes in an instant – they want things to change right away. Life doesn't work that way. It took a long time for you to get to where you are – now you want to change it overnight – it just doesn't happen that way. You are now starting to gain control of your life and instructing your mind and subconscious mind to create opportunities for you to achieve your goals. These opportunities will come to you and you or you will be guided to them. You have to explore these opportunities – not every one of them will be right for you – but you will find the right one and then things will really start to take off.

Who does your dream team consist of? I'm not asking for someone's name, write down the position that he or she would fulfill.

Example: My dream team consists of a customer service assistant to assist with my bookings as well my clients that are enrolled in my coaching program. My branding manager assist with all of my social media platforms and my business strategist assist with revenue generating ideas as well as the revenue that we obtain. This allows me to be free to be creative as well as be available to my clients and customers.

In my personal life my dream team consists of someone I can talk to when I'm frustrated and need to vent. I also need someone that can assist me with my children when things are hectic as well as someone that I can relax with and just be myself.

It's easier to identify what you need a person to do versus identifying who you have in your life that can fulfill the duties that you need someone to fulfill. Often times we get discouraged because we don't have "who" we desire to have in our corner, so we feel defeated before we ever start.

Who do you need to develop your dream team in life?

When thinking about this, think about what your weaknesses are, what you need assistance with and what makes you happy and wanting to continue to move forward. What positions do you need filled?

_____

_____

_____

_____

Who fits the bill?

_____

_____

_____

_____

Who do you need to form your dream team in business?

Remember, sometimes you may have to look on the outside of your "familiar circle" and connect with others that are traveling the same path as you. Think of some support groups as well as ministries that may enable you to stay focused and in motion. It is a must that whoever you put in these positions need to have a knowledge base in what you desire for them to do and is "likable." Nobody wants to deal with someone that they don't like. Just because you "put up" with someone's behavior doesn't mean others will have the same tolerance for them.

What positions do you need filled?

_____

_____

_____

_____

Who fits the bill?

_____

_____

_____

_____

The beautiful thing about developing your dream team is that you have full control over who stays and who goes. I've heard many people say that success is a lonely place, but it doesn't have to be. I believe that success is a place filled with unfamiliar people that you must become acquainted with. Not everyone that you desire to take along with is meant to come along. Prepare for the ones that attempt to make you feel guilty because of your success. Often times when we grow out of places in our life, some of our friends and family may interpret it as being left behind.

Although you know that your intentions are not to leave others behind you have to constantly remind yourself that it's not a place that you desire to remain. There's nothing wrong with wanting more and pursuing your goals so don't allow others that are comfortable and complacent with being where they are convince you to stay stuck in a place that you no longer desire to be.

YOUR SUCCESS IS BEHIND YOUR YES!

CHAPTER FOUR

LOUD WHISPERS AND SILENT CRIES

My journey has been very eventful but yet and still I made it. I wasn't always accepted. I didn't always think much of myself. I was in abusive relationships, went through single parenthood dependent on public and government assistance. I made bad choices one after the other until it became normal to me. I went through a period of homelessness, low self-esteem, NO confidence and thoughts of suicide with several unsuccessful attempts. It wasn't until I hit rock bottom that it dawned on me that I was the only person that could help me. I decided to pick up the pieces, get myself together and become gainfully employed. This afforded me the opportunity to give my children a home and myself a decent car.

After meeting my husband and inheriting a blended family I was in for another tailspin until we were adjusted and acclimated to the changes that were now our new norm. Not long after we were married my baby brother went missing. I mean literally we saw him at my nephews birthday party, he said his goodbye's to everyone as he always did, left with his friend to go to Charlotte, NC for their annual Summer Fest and was never seen again. There was evidence that he came home and left out again. But, what did he leave out for; why was he gone and more importantly why didn't he return? Two and a half agonizing, long dreadful weeks later after we spent endless days and tireless nights searching for him we finally gave up.

With all that I had left in me I cried out to God with a different prayer. I stopped asking him to bring him home safely. After all; I was a nurse I could help take care of him even if he was injured. But something in my spirit wouldn't allow me to continue to wish for something that wouldn't happen. I changed my prayer and asked God for closure. So many families never have closure, never find their loved one and suffer for years if not for the rest of their lives with uncertainties and unanswered questions. So I decided to ask for him to allow us to bring him home so that he could be laid to rest. I knew without a shadow of doubt that he was no longer with us. He would NEVER leave his firstborn and only child for more than thirty minutes without calling and checking to see how she was doing or if she needed anything. He would often call us jokingly and say "I heard my baby call me what she want?" This was one of the most difficult times in my life.

We decided not to look for him and to rest for a day and allow God to work and literally the next day we received a phone call from the local authorities telling us that they had found my brothers body. He had loss control of his car and hydroplaned into the woods where his car was covered with the branches and trees as if he was welcomed and covered in a safe haven until he was found. We weren't able to view his body at his memorial due to the length of time that he was out in nature. But, we were able to reflect on all the memories and good times that we shared with him. Although we were grateful that we were able to have closure for the family, this opened a new chapter for my mom that affected her for the rest of her life.

As if that wasn't enough not even a year later my husband lost his sister to the rare genetic Wilson's disease. Needless to say our life and marriage became challenged through the stress of life changing events, outside interferences and influences and ultimately resulted in us losing our connection with God. Two years into a marriage I found myself wanting out. After numerous counseling sessions, fights and several nights of separation we finally became civil enough to take time to make time to listen to each other and work on rebuilding what was torn down. Things began to go well and then a year later life threw yet another curve ball. I went to visit my mom and greeted her with a hug and kiss as usual and noticed a small knot under her arm. I asked her about it and she said "I noticed it, but I thought it came from a different soap or deodorant I used." Because I knew she had very sensitive skin I didn't think any more of it. At least that was until a couple of weeks went by I noticed that the area had gotten twice the size that it was when I initially saw it.

My sister and I encouraged her to see her primary physician. As a nurse I already knew that she would be asked to go have a biopsy of the knot so that she could be treated accurately. Just as I thought she was seen by the physician and was instructed to have a biopsy. We waited for the results with absolutely no fear or concerns that is until we received them. We went to my mom's follow up appointment and were told that the biopsy showed that the area was malignant. My mom really didn't know what malignant meant. I knew full well what it meant, but I was so numb I couldn't speak. I immediately went into grace mode. I started speaking to her like I always heard her and my dad speak to people who came to the church with their doctors' report. I said "mom no worries, everything will be fine. We'll do what the doctor tells us to do, pray about things and watch things work out."

After going to specialist after specialist searching for a more favorable answer we finally had to come to grips with what was in front of us our mom had stage 4 triple negative breast cancer, one of the most aggressive cancers that a woman could be diagnosed with. Still we held on to our faith and followed the plan of care that she was given.

I continued to work as a director of nursing until I got "the phone call." You know the phone call that changes your world as you once knew it, that phone call. My phone rang. I looked at the caller ID and saw my sister's name. I immediately knew that it had to be about my mom. I asked one of my managers to take over the meeting as I took the call. "KITA" she said in the most heartbroken and desperate voice. I began clearing my desk and packing my bag because I knew it couldn't have been good. Against everything in me I finally responded "what is it?" She told me that the doctor was in to see my mom and I needed to come home immediately. Luckily I had a team of supportive nursing staff that cared so much about me they offered their vacation hours in addition to mine so that I could take the time off I needed to be with my mom.

What was usually a forty-five minute drive took me all of twenty minutes to get there. As I pulled in the parking lot of the hospital it seemed as if the building got larger and I got smaller. My head began to spin, my mouth got so full of saliva that I felt nauseated. The palms of my hands were so sweaty that I had to dry them off. My knees buckled and I felt as if I was going to fall to the ground.

I braced myself by holding on to the door my car. I stood up straight and took three deep breaths. I inhaled one breath through my nose and exhaled through my mouth. I did the several more times and as I exhaled tears began to fall and meet under my chin to the point that the front of my shirt was saturated with tears. Finally, I just had to yell out to relieve the pressure that I felt in my chest. Once I did this I was able to walk without stumbling. I walked into the lobby of the hospital and went to the elevator. My finger was shaking so badly that as I attempted to press the up arrow to open the elevator my finger would slide to the side of the button. I literally had to press the up arrow with my knuckle. The elevator doors opened and I walked onto the elevator whispering a silent prayer to God that things wouldn't be as bad as they seemed. This short elevator ride seemed as if it took an hour. I began to feel claustrophobic and was relieved when the doors finally opened.

As I got off the elevator onto the floor that my mom's room was on it seemed as if everyone knew what was going on but me. The nurses that once approached me with smiling faces and hugs looked at me with a face of pity and made little to no eye contact. My heart began to beat so fast that I began feeling numb on my left side. I began talking to myself so that I would calm down. As I approached the room door I felt stillness and void that gave me chills. I slightly knocked on the door with one hand as I was turning the knob with the other hand and walking in the room at the same time.

As I entered the room I saw the doctor standing at the foot of my mom's bed, my sister standing at my mom's bedside and everyone but the doctor with a blank look on their faces. So I asked "what's going on?" my mom said "he said I don't have but six months" for what I asked? To live, he said I only have six months to live. Being a believer I immediately erased what I just heard from my mind and began speaking life. As a nurse I know the importance of keeping an open mind and upbeat spirit to heal effectively. I submitted my resignation virtually effective immediately. Through this process we watched my mom's once uplifted, positive spirit begin to dwindle into a weak feeble ninety-eight pound body of a woman that began to look unfamiliar to me. Pain replaced her happiness. Hope was replaced with peace and exactly six months after we received the life altering news of her prognosis she took her final breath. My life as I once knew it was over. I no longer desired the things that I once desired because in my mind there was no need. I felt betrayed by God and felt like he let my family down. My father being the pastor of two churches, laboring and working for God being faithful to his word and living "by the book" were all reasons that I felt like God would answer our prayers and heal my mom.

I went months without praying and acknowledging that I was even a believer because of the pain that I felt and the void that I was left with. Reality finally set in that I was a "motherless child." After the rage left and anger subsided I was finally able to feel again and grieve the loss of my mom. I thought about the idea of me being so infuriated with God and realized that I had been in many fights in my life and won most of them, but I was definitely defeated when it came to fighting with God. Since I didn't want to wake up dead I came to my senses and immediately apologized to the Lord so that we could move forward (smile.)

To be perfectly honest I was bitter. I would see people with their mom and become jealous. I would see family and some of my friend's with their mom and think to myself "now the Lord

could have took at least two of them and left my mama alone."
Yea, I know it was a bit much, but I just thought that I would
confess. Emotions are real. Regardless of who you are there will
be a time in your life when your faith is tested. It's so easy to
say what we will do and how we will react to things until they
actually happen.

Several months later my dad was celebrating his 53rd birthday
but his first one without my mom (or as he would call her, "his
sweet baby" in thirty-one years.) I took the liberty to plan a
comedy show celebration to lift his spirits and I decided to put
myself in the mix. It was on that night of September 25th 2010
that magic happened and who you know as Comedian Nikita B
was born. I knew that laughter releases healing endorphins and
as the bible says it's like a medicine and as a nurse I know the
importance of laughter. After the show was over I was
approached by this really nice lady requesting that I come to her
church. She asked "excuse me can I have your booking
information?" I looked around me thinking she has to be talking
to someone else. She then tapped me on my shoulder to make
sure that she had my attention and asked again, "can I have
your booking information? My church would love you she said."
Both shocked and confused I replied to her by saying "I didn't
know I was bookable." She laughed and said "just do what you
did here and you'll be fine;" that one night was the start of an
on the road life style change for me and my family.

Comedy became therapy to me. It wasn't long after my start
that I began to have so many request and engagements that it
interfered with me having a normal "nine-to-five." For the
second time I was thinking of resigning from a six figured salary
position. I had to make a choice and instead of quitting work all
together I decided to go the entrepreneurial route and began to

work as an independent nurse consultant. I also stretched myself and my husband and opened a chain of family care homes in both South and North Carolina. This was a scary adventure, but it proved to be one of the best decisions that we ever made. The business catapulted in ways we couldn't imagine. A lot of foolishness came with it as well, but we'll talk about that later. So here I am again with this unexpected life change. The only difference was I was happy now. I was doing what I loved. I was helping to heal people both on and off the stage and enjoying life as I did it.

Although my mom's death was a tragedy for me it was also the trigger that ignited the comedian, transformational speaker and person you know today. I took the hurt, disappointment, discouragement and all the pain that I had experienced and took it to the stage and left it there. I know how it feels to be hopeless, lost and confused so I've been gracing stages across the country and touching pain points that others are experiencing that may feel like I once did to show them that they can get past it too. T

Thankfully I have strong spiritual foundation and support system and was able to bounce back. But, I'm full aware that not everyone is blessed with those things. It's amazing to me how purpose can be birthed out of your pain. If you think about it there have been times that you may have felt defeated or as if you got the short end of the stick but when the dust settled you were in a much better place than you were before you went through the things that you encountered. We have to remember that things don't happen to us but they happen for us.

As my mom would often say "some things we bring on ourselves" the way we respond to things depicts how we will be responded to. If we have a positive response then usually things will be favorable for us. If we respond negatively then we normally have some unfavorable consequences that we would have to face. Had I continued to look at my mom passing away negatively and ignoring the fact that she no longer was in pain and was finally at peace I would have put myself in a dark place that would have consumed me leaving me worthless to myself or my family.

I will never forget the night that I was finally at peace with my mom passing away. I was having a sleepless night which had become my new norm. I was thinking about my mom and missing her terribly and I began questioning God and just asking "why" the Lord spoke to me and said "I heard your prayer, but I answered hers." It was then that I received instant sense of peace about my mom's transition. Once I finally drifted off to sleep I could hear my mom's voice say to me "I don't know whose daughter you are because any child of mine wouldn't be acting like this. Don't you forget "you are somebody!" When I woke up the next morning I gathered a pen and piece of paper that I kept on my night stand and wrote "because I am somebody."

Later I went back to that same paper and circled the first letter of each word and it spelled "BIAS." This was so significant for me because I would often talk to my mom about not feeling like I was enough and being caught up on my physical appearance and thinking I wasn't pretty enough. Having been looked over and denied for things for other biased reasons, I decided to take what was known to others as a negative word with negative meaning and give it a new meaning of positivity and significance. This taught me the power of positive thinking. Now here I was trying to put the pieces back together. I made up in my mind that I wouldn't procrastinate on any of my other dreams because life had no guarantees and we never knew what day would be the last.

What are the 3 TOP things that you have had to overcome?

1)

2)

3)

Guess what, if you're reading this book YOU DID IT! Even if
you struggle with the aftermath of it at times, you're still here
and you made it. Silence the small voice that keeps trying to talk
you into reliving the negative things that you've overcome.
Speak the truth out loud each time you are minded about the
things you experienced. Know that you are not responsible for
someone else's faults. We all have the power of choice; it's up
to each of us to make the right ones.

If you need to forgive someone forgive them. You're not giving
them permission to hurt you again, but you're giving yourself
permission to love again. If you need to forgive yourself, do so.
Sometimes you have to accept the fact that others may not
accept your apology regardless of how sincere you may be.

CHAPTER FIVE

MATTERS OF THE HEART

One of the other fears that I hear others talk about is the fear of not having support. Whenever you're motivated to move forward and have experienced some successes you may see some changes in your family and friends. Like any caring person you want to take as many people along with you as possible, but you'll quickly learn that everyone isn't ready for elevation. Like the old saying goes "you can't take everyone with you." When you acknowledge the fact that you can't be successful alone and then realize that you don't have many people in your circle that's equipped to support you fear finds a way to creep it's ugly head back in the equation.

We experienced this couple of years after my mom passed. Our business is expanding. I added a home health business in the mix and I was building and expanding my brand. I've hired a team of professionals so that I continue moving forward in a positive was and *life is good!* That's until we had another life change to happen. We had a nephew to come spend the night and well let's just say that morning has yet to come three years later. My girls have become divas and my boys are doing any and everything that they think they're bad enough to do. Everybody was trying to fit in with somebody and be a part of something. I literally felt as if I was in a house of strangers. Things got to be so overwhelming that I just threw my hands up and wanted to give up. I mean my goodness, I've lost my mom, my children are acting a monkey and now I'm an instant mom again and everybody is looking for me to be super woman while they acted as if they were super stupid. Really? I finally decided to go seek counseling and finally I got frustrated talking to someone on a weekly basis about people that should be there receiving services themselves. I loved my family, but I didn't like them at all. I know that may sound harsh, but I can promise you that someone reading this was wondering if it was normal to feel this way so let me be the first to tell you that you are not alone. Great news is it does get better.

Even though I had these unforeseen changes happen to me life for me couldn't have been any better. My family was secure, we didn't have to ask or want for anything. Everything was a fingertip away. That was until it was all taken away from us. After telling my daughter that she couldn't go to the local skating rink at least seventy-five times on try number seventy-six something spoke to me and told me to let her go. Hesitantly I said "Yes." But luckily I made the choice to change my mind. Upon our return home we saw cop cars, an ambulance and the local fire department. No knowing what was going on I did what any caring parent would do, I turned to make sure that the kids still had their seatbelts on so we wouldn't get a ticket trying to get through the chaos.

We decided to go home the back way to see if we could get a better look at things. We weren't prepared for what we saw; our home was in flames in front of our eyes. Smoke was barreling so thick that were unable to see our hands in front of us. Both firefighters and crisis center representatives approached us wanting to make sure that nobody was left in the home. Our son wanted to stay home and sleep thanks to God we made him ride with us to pick my daughter up. As I sit back and think about it, if we would have allowed him to stay that may have been the last time we saw him alive. From that point on I've always listened to my gut.

So now here I am a wife, mother of five and a possible, entrepreneur and comic at a place of familiarity. One that I promised self-time after time again that I would not visit again. I had to make a conscious decision. Would I take my family through the unpredictable stages that depression took you through or would I take an alternate route? Since I knew how I felt when I was in that dark place in my life and knew I didn't want to revisit it again I made a choice; I chose to be happy! Why? I'm glad you asked. I chose happiness because I believed that I mattered. I knew that in order for me to live, laugh and prosper I had to first address matters of the heart. I always like to bring a witness with me and give examples of others that had similar experiences (I think that's the Southern Baptist in me.)

In this book I like to read there is a story of a lame man that was lame from birth. So we know that this man has never walked or been able to care for himself. He has had men carry him at the gate called "beautiful" everyday so that he could ask for alms. In our day and time we would consider him a bomb or a beggar. They would place him in front of this particular gate because it was the entrance way into the temple. Just as most of us would think, so did this man. He thought that if he would ask the believers or as some of us may say the saints then he would be okay. Have you ever been in that kind of situation? Depending on someone that you felt would be there for you, or hoping that someone would see your need? Imagine this guy going to the same place at the same time continuously seeking the assistance and support of others. He did all he knew to do by asking for alms from people that he thought would share with him. This would allow him to have his needs met and I wouldn't doubt that he even shared with his family. It never says how long the man did this, but what we do know is he was born with this condition and now as a grown man he was being carried to do what was familiar with him.

I wouldn't doubt that he did this even as a child. After all; what caring person can deny a helpless child? So for years he has done this repetitive thing day after day to survive. That was until he met Peter and John. As he sat in front of the gate called "beautiful" at the entrance of the temple he saw both Peter and James. Without hesitation he asked them for alms. Peter looked at his partner John and looked at the lame man and said "look at me." The lame man looked at him and Peter said "silver and gold have I not, but what I do have I'll give to you." He asked the lame man, "Do you want to walk" he replied "yes." Peter said "in the name of Jesus of Nazareth…….." He reached and grabbed the man by his right hand and helped him to stand. The man gained strength in his ankle bone…… realizing that he was standing the man followed Peter and John into the temple. He walked, leaped and praised God for the miracle that he had just experienced. People looked at him in amazement because everybody knew that he was the lame man that they passed every morning as they entered into the temple.

Now let's look at things for a moment. This man was born in a situation that he had no control over. He had two choices. He could play the cards that he was dealt, or he could complain about his situation, blame others and even worst give up. We all know that everyone isn't acceptable and the others aren't so nice. Think of the names he may have been called the treatment that he may have received. During this era if you were born with any disabilities or abnormal in any way, you were looked upon as sinful and many times cast out. You were considered to be a "nobody" because you were dependent upon others to ensure you survived. Because begging may have been all that this man and his family knew would benefit them him and them he was encouraged to continue to do so. I can imagine that he heard things like "this is the only way you'll be able to take care of yourself, you'll never walk and be like everyone else, nobody will ever believe in you." Sounds harsh huh? But, this is the reality for so many people and you may have even experienced it yourself. Because they were born into a situation or faced with uncontrollable circumstances they were told that they had no other choice but to accept it. Some situations may even be hereditary and because your relative has gone through certain things you've been persuaded that you would have to travel that same road. The lame man listened to the people that surrounded him and took the instructions of those that thought they knew was best for him. He believed the things that he heard and listened to the naysayers, haters and nonbelievers and expected to be in the same situation for the rest of his life.

He expected to go have someone carry him in front of the temple so that he could ask for alms as he usually did. He also expected to receive alms by the people he reached out to but, little did he know that his expectations would be altered when he met Peter and John. This was nothing that the lame man was proud of doing as evidence by him not making eye contact with Peter when he asked for alms. Peter had to give him instructions to look at him. So even in shame he still did what he thought he needed to do in order to survive. To his amazement he got more than he bargained for. Peter offered him something he probably silently prayed for ever since he was old enough to understand. He offered him the ability to be normal, something that he had never experienced; to think even further than that he would not be dependent upon anyone else. His expectations were immediately altered. No longer was he concerned about receiving any type of alms because he was getting some much more valuable. No doubt in my mind doubt, fear and disbelief were trying to attack his confidence, but without hesitation when Peter asked him if he wanted to walk he said "YES!" Peter having faith that through God he was healed he immediately stretched his hand out and assisted him to stand.

Now that his expectations were altered it was up to him to understand that his condition had changed. He had to know that there was an alteration in the things that he once knew as normal and that his life would never be the same. After these things were revealed to him and he saw for himself that he was actually standing, something that he hadn't did in his entire life he had to make the decision to take the "big step." Literally, he had to take a step to believe that this new revelation was true. Not only did he take a step, but he leaped. Then with excitement, thankfulness and no regard to the people around him he shouted as loud as he could and began praising God for what he had done in his life.

Even if you don't share my beliefs or read the book that I love to read I want you to look at the significance of the lame man's life. He heard so many different things in his life that affected the way that he saw himself. He listened to people who only saw him at his current state and had no faith that things would or could change for him. He expected to always have to depend on others to carry him to his destinations as well as give him the things that he needed. When his expectations were altered he immediately changed how he saw himself. His mindset changed about who he could become.

When Peter assisted him to stand and he felt the strength in his ankles and feet he received the revelation that he too could do what everyone else around him could do. Notice that he had to first have someone in his corner that believed in his ability just as much as he did. Please don't miss the lesson tin this revelation. In order for you to do something you've never done and be the person you know you're designed to be you have to first separate yourself from the naysayers, haters and doubters that pour negative energy into your life and refuse to see your best potential.

Even when the lame man could see what was revealed to him it wasn't until he actually took the "BIG STEP" that his transformation actually begins. Too many times we go through the process of identifying the things that we want and allow outside interferences to detour us from them and never pursue what it was we desired to pursue. Even when we do push forward and see the things that we must do and change we don't do it. Simply put we become stuck. Life happens and we somehow forget all the things we've always desired and aspired to do. But, ironically enough we are constantly reminded of all the negative talk and self-doubt that we replay in our heads over and over again.

H(earing)- What and who are you listening to?

_____

_____

If they're not building you up then they're tearing you down!

E(xpectation)- What are you expecting for yourself? Don't base
this on what you see in front of you, but on your desired outcome.

_____

_____

_____

A(lteration)- What changes do you need to make to be successful?

Changes that need to be made?

_____

_____

Places you need to STOP going to

_____

_____

Places you need to start going to

_____

_____

People you need to disassociate yourself with (even if it's family
or friends)

_____

_____

_____

People you need to start associating yourself with

_____

_____

R(evelation)-What was revealed to you before "life happened?"

_____

_____

Transformation will NOT happened until you hear the right things, expect more, alter and change what needs to changed!

What concerns you also concerns God! He will give you the desires of your heart, but we have to make sure that the things that we keep in are heart is pure in desire and intent.

Psalms 37:4 Delight thyself also in the lord and he shall give thee the desires of thine heart.

CHAPTER SIX

THE FEAR OF BEING ALONE

You have to always understand and realize that we are all purposefully created. There is great in all of us but sadly enough not all of us tap into that greatness for one reason or another. If we could only think as a child and have no doubt, ignore all negativity and anyone that tells us that we can't do something and just go for it things would be so much better. Instead we hold on to things that may have been told to us as a child and process it as truth and put up a mental wall of defeat and refuse to try. You may not be lame in the way the lame man that couldn't walk is, but there is something in your life that has you paralyzed.

I don't know if this is a mental, spiritual or physical paralysis for you, but I can assure you that you have become stagnate by it. If I don't know anything else I know that life happens and when it does you have to learn to both deal and live with it. The country singer Willie Rogers sang a song about a card game, but the words are so profound. The words were "you have to know when to fold them, know when to hold them, know when to walk away, know when to run." Even though he was references a card game you can apply this same method to your life. When it deals you a hand you whether it's a good or bad one you have to play it. You have to know when to hold them; are the things you're doing working for you and are the people associated with you really for you? After you've determined that know that those are the things and people that you must hold on to. You have to know when to fold them.

What and who do you have in your life that no longer serves you any purpose and brings no value to you? Do you have things that you are investing in that you hardly touch? If so it's time to fold it. Let it go. You have to know when to walk away. I'm sure you've heard this before; "doing the same thing expecting different results is the definition of insanity." So what things are driving you crazy? Are you investing valuable time in something or someone that is sucking you dry? You're trying to make things work by showing your faithfulness and willingness to go all in, but you're not getting even half of this same effort in return. Well, as hurtful as this is to hear it's time to walk away. Then you have those toxic relationships, bad habits and unhealthy behaviors that you know without a shadow of doubt that you should've stopped long before now. Needless to say it's time to run with no looking back. There's no need to compare your situation to others or make excuses for where you are.

It's time that you take ownership and understand that you are responsible for yourself. There may have been some unfortunate things that happened to you that you can't seem to let go, but you have to find a way to move on. Time is out for you harboring forgiveness and hatred towards the people and things that you feel have harmed you in one way or another. While you are allowing these negative things to physically, emotionally and mentally harm you the person or people have moved on with their life and has taken no regard to the way you feel.

Not letting go is like drinking poison and expecting the people around you to die from it. It just won't happen. It's almost impossible to discover your purpose when you are allowing things from your past to occupy your mind, heart and spirit. If you are having a difficult time finding your purpose or don't believe that you have a purpose for your life; simply think about that thing that you are great at. Think about what brings you the most happiness, what do people ask you to do for them all the time? The thing that comes naturally to you that you would do or have done at no cost because you love it just that much. When you think of the things that people always tell you, what are the words that they use to describe you? Think about these things and write them down. Ask God to give you clarity on the purpose he has for you to do.

We sometimes think that we aren't good enough, smart enough or whatever else enough to do that thing that is tugging at you that you can't seem to stop thinking about. I can attest to you that it's that tug that's trying to direct you and its called purpose. Stop ignoring the recurring soft voice that is trying to lead you in the right direction. If you would change your thoughts and beliefs in your inner world then you change the reality in your outer world. You have to remember that your subconscious mind is always at work. It's continuously shaping and creating your life. It responds to your thoughts and beliefs so you must remember that your subconscious mind doesn't know if you're "just kidding" so you should always speak, believe and think positive thoughts when it's pertaining to you and your life. You have to give your thoughts and beliefs direction. You have to conquer both fear and anxiety. These emotions will always come to you whenever you decide to make a change in your life.

Fear and anxiety are at times indicators that you're not prepared for what it is that you want to do. Your mind will try to convince you that you don't need to change or do the things that you desire to do because it doesn't want to be uncomfortable, it is comfortable where you are right now, even if you aren't happy. You have to become the change that you want to see. You have to quiet the mind, or as my dad would always tell me "kill the stinking thinking!" Put the negative things of your past behind you. The only thing that matters now is how you view yourself right now. You can be successful and it's your responsibility to succeed.

Don't let others influence you with their negative views. Expect people to tell you how crazy your ideas are and try to talk you out of them. But, replace that negativity with positive thoughts and take action. The more you focus on things that you want to change the closer you'll get to accomplish those things. It's always easier to stay where you are than to change. But, you have to remember that is you don't change nothing else will. You must believe in yourself and your abilities.

Isolation is the enemy's platform for you. This is a place that he can convince you of every lie that you've struggled to overcome. It's pertinent that you surround yourself with people that assist you with staying focused, fluent as well as productive.

Who can you gleam from in your area of potential growth?

_____

_____

_____

_____

_____

_____

_____

_____

What groups or organizations can you join that will assist you with accountability as well as enable you to network with others that will assist you building your net worth?

_____

_____

_____

_____

_____

_____

_____

_____

_____

_____

_____

CHAPTER SEVEN

THE I AM FACTOR

Once you conquer this belief that you can accomplish anything you want and adopt the method of continuously viewing yourself in a positive light regardless of what others may say you will see the universe deliver those things to you. This is the same method of "the laws of attraction." I'm sure you've heard the saying "what goes around comes around." This statement is so true, but you are responsible for the things that come to you. You must take control of your life and direct you inner powers and subconscious mind. This may sound like you're a super hero, but is you think about it you actually are. You are here to save the day. By saving your day today you'll be creating the success for your tomorrow. You will always have a mental tug of war whenever you desire change or want more, but the great thing about that is you have all the power! You have the power to create the life you want. Your mind is like a garden and just like a garden you can either neglect or cultivate it.

If you had a physical garden and weeds grew in it if you didn't remove them and care for your garden the weeds would ruin everything. Well your mind is your garden and small thinking, worry fear, doubt, poor choices and lack of confidence are all weeds. If you don't remove those weeds from your mind they will spread like wildfire and consume all your positive thoughts, ambition and desire for more leaving you in ruins. When you get to this point in our mind we automatically feel defeated and want to give up even though even though you know you need to continue. Then things get worst. When you're filled with negative beliefs and negative thinking subconsciously your inner belies and spirit man will create more negative situations.

Things in turn will create more and more of what you don't want. Your life continues to get worst. You believe it will never get better. Life becomes more difficult. You want change but can't seem to turn things around. Does this sound like you? If this is you then you are allowing your negative thought patterns and beliefs to spread.

You are what you think you are and however you perceive yourself is how others will see you as well. When life has dealt you a tough hand and you have so many things that are against you and you feel like giving up, it's then that you are closer than you've ever been to reaching your goal and or receiving your breakthrough. When you're in the darkest places of your life and you can't seem to figure a thing out that's usually where your gift lies. It wasn't until I lost my mom and had all of these shattered pieces of my heart and mind surrounding me that I discovered my gift of comedy. It was at a time that I was determined not to revisit that place of depression, sadness and grief and to do something uplifting, inspiring and motivational that would change my life for the rest of my life. Buried under pain, hurt, anger, rage, bitterness, resentment and other negative emptions was laughter, happiness and joy.

Once I was able to see how to make those things possible in my life and the life of those around me I was able to discover my "hidden gift." Who would have known that behind the death of my mom and after going through one of the toughest times of my life that I would have it as a catalyst to my success? Had I not gone through the things that I experienced I may have never developed into the person that I am today and probably wouldn't have reached as any people as I've reached. So, just as I have discovered my hidden gift so can you. To close family and friends it wasn't a shock to them that I was a comedian.

According to them I was always able to change the setting or tone in the atmosphere. I have always been able to make people smile and laugh at things that they normally would have been upset about. The gift was always there, but it took something happening for it to be revealed. Although I hate that it was through the death of my mom, I'm glad to have finally found my purpose. I pray you won't have to experience death in order to find your missing link or your purpose. But, I'm also cheering for you that you're able to identify your purpose and experience the joy that you deserve. I'm a witness that there's joy in progress.

Think about the place that you're in right now. Think about the way that you feel and the things, experiences and circumstances that got you to that place. Now that you can visualize those things I want you to imagine what it would take for you to make your situation better. Regardless of what it may cost, the friends you may have to loss, the family you may have to love from a distance or the changes that you will have to make. What would you have to do in order to make life better for you? Now what are the steps that you will have to take in order to get there? See how easy that was? A lot of times we make things difficult for us because we don't want to make the necessary changes in order to develop and deliver like we should. Believe it or not your gift is hidden underneath all of the rubble and debris of the left over things that you've been left with after life threw you a curve ball. Think back to those things that you do well naturally. Think about the things that people either ask you to do, ask for your advice about or that you would do for free simply because you enjoy it so much. When you think of those things then think of the reason why you're not doing it.

What has hidden covered or buried your desire to pursue the things that makes you happy and enables you to serve others. What circumstance or person has so much influence on you that you have decided to allow it to cost you your happiness? Everybody has a gift but not everyone will discover it simply because we won't take out the time to search through the debris and residue to find it. Maybe you are really great with your hands and you make things, you build things for people or you sew and design things for yourself and others. You may be a really good cook and have people request you make signature dishes or you're known for certain desserts. You may even be a phenomenal hairstylist and always wanted to do bigger things like have your own product line or own your own shop. Maybe you specialize in natural hair and have special tips and tricks on how to be a natural beauty. Maybe you have a beautiful voice and you're always asked to sing, or you've recorded a cd and maybe even entertained the thought of pursuing it full time. Maybe you're a speaker, or a comic I mean the possibilities are endless.

You may be a walking wealth of knowledge. You know how to get things done easier, more proficient and cost effective and are always trouble shooting things for people. Speaking of fixing things maybe you are known as "Mr. Fix It" or you are gifted to fix cars or you are a great electrician and you enjoy doing it, but you haven't went any further because it would require you to further your education, invest more time and money or you just simply haven't done it. Well these are just a few things, but all of them are things that people are gifted with naturally that they may have picked up on, saw others do or was intrigued by them and learned more about it. But, yet and still this is not what they are doing. They are spending their time and effort using their talents to build someone else's dream instead of operating in their gift and building their dreams and a life that they love.

Some people say they don't know what their gift is and that's just simply not true. Again, what is it that you do really well, that people ask you about or ask you to do all the time? What is that thing that you would do for free because you enjoy it so much, or that thing that you never went to school to learn to do but you do exceptionally well? Have you thought about it, well there's your gift? And the burning desire, the tug in your spirit or the continuous thought of doing it is your passion to pursue your purpose. Imagine this you're at the start line and your gift and purpose is at the finish line. But, in between you and your gift are obstacles, worry, confusion, work, battles, naysayers, haters and whatever else that have kept you from reaching your destination. You have all of these things that have hidden your true gift and are enabling you to walk in your purpose.

Often times we cloud our minds with so many possibilities that it paralyzes us and stops us from being able to make a decision. So once you've identified what it is you desire to do that will have you in alignment with your purpose identify what it is buried under and establish the steps that need to be taken in order to reveal your gift and allow you to move forward. The bible tells us that our gift will make room for us and have us before great men. So if you feel stagnate and unfulfilled in the current place that you're in it may not be because you need to be challenged more. It may be simply because you're operating in your talent instead of in your gift. Once you've identified what your gift is or what it is that God is calling you to do; you need to do that one thing, NOT everything but that one thing.

Not everyone has the desire to be an entrepreneur or establish a business of their own. Some people can operate in their gift and that's fine. But, to the ones that desire more there is more out there you just have to be willing to dig through the rubble and seek God for clarity. Possibilities are endless and opportunity awaits you once you make up your mind that you're ready to reveal your hidden gift. Once you discover the "I Am" that resides within you everything else will fall into place.

"I AM" are the two most powerful words that you will ever speak out of your mouth. These words are affirming as well as your belief system spoken out loud. Regardless of what you may be feeling or what may have been spoken to you, it is pertinent that you only speak positive, uplifting and positive words over yourself.

Example: (My favorite) I AM SOMEBODY! I AM HEALTHY! I AM PROSPEROUS! I AM HIGHLY SOUGHT AFTER TO SPEAK TO THE MASSES! I AM A COACH THAT ONLY HAS PROSPEROUS CLIENTS! I AM BOOKED ALL YEAR LONG! I AM SEEN ON MEDIA OUTLETS ALL OVER THE WORLD! I AM A MILLIONAIRE!

See how I affirm my desired outcomes. Speak as if it is already done. DO NOT use any negative words (try, may, think, going to etc.)

List 10 affirmations that you can speak out loud on a daily basis to help you with your mindset prep.

1)

2)

3)

4)

5)

6)

7)

8)

9)

10)

Now that you have these written out, record yourself saying these things out loud. Place these things in places where they are visible to you (i.e.; on your mirror, on your dashboard, on your home page on your computer and or cell phone etc.)

CHAPTER EIGHT

SOMETIMES YOU HAVE TO BRING THE "B" OUT OF YOU!

I know what you're thinking and just life the title of the book; I'm not dropping any bombs on you. I'm not telling you to bring the "B" out of you that will cause you to repent. I'm talking about BOLDNESS! In order for you to conquer fear you have to face it and by facing it I mean looking whatever it is eye to eye and taking it head on. You have to know who you are and what you're called to do. Being bold doesn't mean you're being mean, arrogant or rude. It simply means that you have the confidence that you need to face the things that you need to face. It means that because you know who you are you will stand in your truth and not allow others to dictate to you who you are.

You have to be bold in your life. When things challenge you that you may be intimidated by you must be bold enough to face it. When you have toxic people in your life you must be bold enough to cut them off. Even if those people are family, it doesn't mean that you don't love them it simply means that you recognize that their season is over in your life. Their voice and information has expired. You have to be bold in your business. Whether or not you're an entrepreneur or an employee you still need to possess boldness.

You have to be bold enough to apply for that promotion, stand firm in your decisions and lead as you were born to do. Without boldness you won't step up to the plate when it's your turn to be served. You have to set boundaries. In life you have to set boundaries for the people close to you as well as the people that frequent your space. You can't allow yourself to waste time in things that drain your energy. You have to put boundaries on EVERYTHING! You have to put boundaries on the actions that you allow your children to exhibit if not what may have made you laugh at one point will embarrass you later. You must have boundaries or shall I say compromises with your partner or spouse that will allow you both to live in peace and harmony. You have to have boundaries to stay in a place of solitude as well as structure.

In business you have to have boundaries. You have to show up to work on time, come back from lunch on time as well as give your best efforts and services whenever you are being of service for others. The cliché "he may not come when you want him, but he's always on time" doesn't apply to you. Stop your "almost being late" syndrome every morning when you have to report to work. You talking about "I might not be here when you want me, but I'm on time. Chile, if you don't hush! Get yourself together and establish yourself some boundaries.

Self-control is the first cousin to boundaries. You can't have one without the other. You must exhibit self-control so that you can set the boundaries that are needed in order for you to be successful. Then you need the big "B." You have to BELIEVE! Your belief system is the determining factor that determines how far you get in any space that you operate in. What do you believe for yourself? How do you view yourself? It doesn't know matter how much we know about something if you don't believe that you can do it then it will never get done. If you don't believe that your life can be grand then it won't be. If you don't believe you'll get the promotion you want then you will not. Whatever you tell yourself you will definitely believe it. So I ask you, what do you believe?

What are you afraid of? What have you allowed fear to keep you from accomplishing? The time is now for you to beat the "F" out of fear and activate your faith. Even though you can't see it right now you have to have the faith that you will be able to accomplish the things that you have set out to accomplish. You have to focus on the promise and not the problem. Yes it may look like one thing, but you have to keep the end in mind. Maybe you don't know all the steps, so what. You don't have to know all the steps. You only need to take one step at a time and if you stumble, you have to be bold enough to pick yourself back up! Fear has paralyzed you long enough. It's time for you to dream again. Take fear and jump with it. Faith it until you make it. Please understand that your time is now. Someone else's breakthrough is contingent on you operating in your purpose.

What areas do you need to show more boldness in?

_____

_____

_____

_____

What is your belief system?

I believe in my ability to

_____

_____

_____

_____

I believe that I can assist others to achieve an outcome of

_____

_____

_____

_____

CHAPTER NINE

THE BENEFITS OF FEAR

Contrary to belief fear is not always your enemy. The truth of the matter is most of us are using fear in a non-beneficial way that stunts our growth. If we use the benefits of fear it can be the voice of reason, caution, and practicality that serves you well at times. It takes energy to resist fear. Getting to know it and allowing it to be what it is lets your body and mind relax, as the fight to overcome it is over. This opens the space for creativity, wonder, awe, love, beauty and inspiration. If you haven't learned by now, running from fear doesn't work. If we avoid facing it, it will always be nipping at your heels forever. Whether you know it or not we all live a fear-led life, choosing our partners, jobs, friends, letting go and making transitions are all done out of fear. Habits and addictions run wild because we are afraid of meeting our feelings. We feel like we're alone and separated; all while alienating ourselves from others, while deep inside, we recognize the still small voice whispering our truths to us.

The benefit to fear is that once you know yourself and what you really desire, fear has a way of making you aware of the warning signs of danger as well as tap into your discernment to assist you with avoiding bad decisions. The beautiful thing about fear is that you can easily determine whether or not it's something you're being guided to avoid or if it's your inner fears trying to stop you from moving forward. Fear speaks in "can not's" but God only speaks in "can's." When fear motivates your thoughts they create negative, imaginary scenarios about the future. Here's the truth; we don't know what the future holds but we know who holds our future. When we create fearful scenarios about what will happen in our future not only are they not true, but they are also limiting to our growth. If you can ignore them or disregard them then you will see that there was no truth to any of it.

The biggest benefit to experiencing fear is that it's designed to keep you safe and limited. The issue is we allow it to keep us so safe that we become paralyzed and don't move at all. When we recognize fear for what it is we can train ourselves to channel that energy of fear into excitement and enthusiasm. If you don't learn to channel fear in this way it will make us think that something negative will happen. Truth of the matter is we don't really know what will happen. We have to become comfortable with not knowing everything about our process so that so that rule doesn't rule you.

One of the biggest mistakes that we make as it pertains to fear is that if we ignore it, it will go away. When in reality resisting fear actually strengthens it. The antidote to conquering fear is being aware of it. You have to be willing to face fear in that moment in order to fully understand the thoughts you have and the physical sensation that you feel so that you can positively recognize it when it rears its head again.

I know that you've learned that God didn't give us the spirit of fear and he didn't. However; we face it all too often. Although we can't get rid of fear we do have the power to change the way you relate to it. Don't feel like something is wrong with you or that you have failed if fear continues to appear. Simply meet it with curiosity and a loving heart so that you can identify the way it shrinks your big ideas, goals and aspirations. Fear is usually heightened after you think about something that you'd love to do. Think about it after you have a great idea or think about your dreams, shortly after you'll start thinking of reasons why you can't or shouldn't do it. Recognizing fear for what it is allows you to make conscious decisions. The benefit to it is that with it you will have the clarity you need to see what fear is guiding you to do, and you can consider what you really want.

3 questions you need to ask yourself when you start to become apprehensive about making decisions to determine if you have fear working against you or if fear is being your friend.

1) Will this decision put me in a predicament or cause harm to me or others?

2) Are my thoughts speaking in "can's or can not's?" Remember God speaks in can's...........

3) If I don't do this will it continue to hinder me from achieving my goal?

After you answer these questions ask yourself this "is this worth me staying stuck where I am?" If your answer is no to this bonus question then fear is not being your friend. Use the techniques discussed to conquer your fear and move forward and pursue your happiness.

CHAPTER TEN

FAITHING IT UNTIL YOU MAKE IT

The presence of fear is a clear indication that you're trusting in your own strengths rather than those of God. Over the years, I've saw how people have allowed fear to hold them back. Fear has kept people from applying for certain jobs, starting a new business, having a difficult conversation, taking a chance or trying something new. But fear can also be an indicator that you want something more……something different…….something better. Rarely do you feel fear when you're in your comfort zone. It's only when you start thinking about making a change- a shift- that could move you closer to your vision and goals does fear rise up in you. If you are feeling stuck because you're in fear the unfortunate truth is that you will probably stay stuck until you are willing to face the fear and move forward anyway. And if you're willing, the next question you have to answer is how do you do it? How so you face it?

The answer is one word "action." You have to face fear and take action and you do this through faith. See when you beat the "F" out of fear, all you have left is "ear." It's no coincidence that faith comes by hearing and hearing the word of God. You have to increase your faith to conquer fear. You must start doing things that challenges your fear. Each time you do something to challenge it each action will help you reduce fear and take positive steps towards your goals. You have to expect more for yourself. Don't look at your current situation and depict your future from where you are. Your vision needs to be so big that it's bigger than your fear.

The bible tells us to write the vision and make it plain. We must do this so that we can see what we truly want every day as a reminder that you must face your dear or be willing to live without your vision. Plan to win! Know exactly what you'll get, have, accomplish or receive IF you move past your fear. When you can clearly see how accomplishing your goals will change your life, your family, your fulfillment, your happiness, your finances, your community, or the world, it becomes unbearable not to act on it. It becomes painful to do nothing.

Having a vision alone is not enough. You must know what your goals are that you need to work on to get that vision that you see for yourself. What steps do you need to take and how do you get there. What do you need to know or learn? There is no reason to live in the unknown. Knowledge diminishes fear and builds confidence. No matter what you accomplish in life, what you accomplish or what you do, whenever you are ready to move forward to a new level or try something different fear will show up. Fear will never go away. I repeat again, the worst mistake you can ever make is to wait for fear to go away. If you do, you'll never move beyond where you are today. So again get used to it.

What you must remember is we were all born with a purpose as well as a gift. Not everybody will use theirs, but they both reside on the inside of us. I work with creatives and aspiring consultants that desire to profit from their expertise every day. When I speak to my clients I let them know that in order to pursue their purpose they must first be clear as to what it is. A confused mind does absolutely nothing! You have to be clear about who you are, what your purpose is and who you're here to serve. Once this is established you then have to build yourself and your brand so that you can position yourself as an expert.

Lastly, you have to increase your visibility so that your audience and people that you are here to serve know where to find you. You must pursue, position and profit. I like to call it "The 3 P's to profiting from your greatness." None of these things can be done as long as you allow fear to stand in the way of you giving yourself an opportunity to win. Stop giving up on yourself before you give yourself an opportunity to try. Stop feeling obligated to be everything to everybody. Once you decide to stop building other people's dreams and build your own, you can't consume yourself with what someone else will have to do in your absence. The same people you're so concerned about leaving because you think they can't function without you; will find someone to replace you before the week is out.

You also have to be delivered from people. You worry about what people say, you worry about what people will think and you worry about if people will take you serious. Truth is not everyone will. The sweet thing about not being caught up with the stigma of others is that you're not here for everyone. So for those you're designed for you will reach and all of the naysayers, non-believers and not so genuine followers will be just fine. Besides, every winning team has cheerleaders as well as spectators. It's your job to clearly define who they are.

I've always heard that fear was "false evidence appearing real." If this is so and you're seeing things for what they aren't, I want you to make the decision to no longer focus on the "can not's" but the "can's." Look at what you can do, think about what you do know and complete the things that you can do. Meanwhile; you find someone doing what you desire to do and is already successful. I learned through one of my mentors that knowledge equals power and power equals profit. This was something I always kept in the back of my mind and it proved to be true as well. When I think back on the times I was successful it was after I was directed by a mentor, invested in myself and learned new strategies or held accountable by an accountability partner. The same way I went through this process is the same way you can as well. I often said that fear was the worst thing that you can live with, but I've found out that it's not. Regret is the worst thing to live with. You have so many aspirations yet fear has stopped you from going any further. After a while you are no longer thinking about fear it's the regret that you toil with because you never tried. So what if you fail at something, I'm sure it won't be the first time you've ever failed in life. Learn the lesson that was intended for you and keep moving.

It may be difficult and sometimes even painful, but if you're going through hell; keep going. I too went through the unpredictable stages of fear, but because I didn't give up I failed my way to success. Everybody's road is different so there's no need of comparing yourself to anyone else. You have no idea what that person went through or endured to get where they are. Understand that when other people try to talk you out of things and don't understand you, they too are speaking from a place of fear. Your success is behind your yes. So until you give yourself permission to be successful you never will be. It's time for you to LAUNCH YOUR DREAMS!

As I always tell you "you are somebody, so am I. The Lord loves you and so do I." Follow me, NOT in your car but on face book (Nikita B Williams) follow me on Instagram, periscope and twitter @iamnikitab Let's stay connected and grow together. If you want to learn more on believing in your abilities, building your dreams and experiencing joy in every area of your life go to: www.nikitabwilliams.com

I DECIDED TO

WALK IN PURPOSE, ON PURPOSE,
FOR·MY PURPOSE AND MYLIFE HASN'T
BEEN THE SAME SINCE!

I'M YOUR #PurposePusher!
#HopeDealer! And
#JoySpecialist!

COMEDIAN *nikita B*

"AH-HA" MOMENTS are those ideas, inspiration and revelations that come to mind whenever you read this book or hear something that gives you more insight on things. Use the following pages to record your take a way's. You must write the vision and make it plain. The quickest way to conquer fear is to face it. Once you face your fears you'll need direction to go the distance. I pray that this book blessed you and helped you look at things differently. There is greatness on the inside of you and its waiting on you to release it.

"AH-HA" MOMENTS

_____

_____

_____

_____

_____

_____

_____

_____

_____

_____

_____

_____

_____

_____

_____

_____

_____

_____

"AH-HA" MOMENTS

"AH-HA" MOMENTS

"AH-HA" MOMENTS

ABOUT THE AUTHOR

nikita B embodies a no-nonsense approach in her message and teaching style entangled with humor in a way that only she can intertwine the two. Outspoken, fiery, transparent and truthful are just a few of the common adjectives used when describing her. After the untimely death of her mother to breast cancer Nikita left her corporate position as a clinical nurse consultant and began her career as a comedian. Uncertain of where this would take her she was determined to reach the masses in hopes to help mend broken hearts and ease troubled minds through laughter.

A former director of nursing turn nationally known comedienne turn expert speaker turn brand business strategist, Nikita has graced many large platforms with many award winning artist. Nikita has won numerous awards and has established herself as an expert in the business and healthcare arenas. Nikita has graced many stages in the faith based arena, colleges, healthcare corporations, leadership institutes as well as other leading agencies.

Nikita established a nonprofit organization (The BIAS Group) composed of individuals of law enforcement, clergy, healthcare, mental health and social services in efforts to service not only the struggling child, but the individuals that compose of his/her support system; In efforts to build a better community and stimulate the economy. Through the BIAS Movement she's changing lives, one mindset at a time.

~Join the movement   www.thebiasmovement.com

IF FEAR HAS BEEN A WAY OF LIFE FOR YOU AND YOU'VE BEEN STUCK IN A PLACE OF OVERWHELM, CONFUSION AND LACK THE STRATEGIES YOU NEED FOR SUCCESS, THEN THIS BOOK IS FOR YOU! #FearNoMore! #Fearless! #NoLimits!

NIKITA HAS BEEN FEATURED ON THE FOLLOWING MEDIA
OUTLETS & MORE

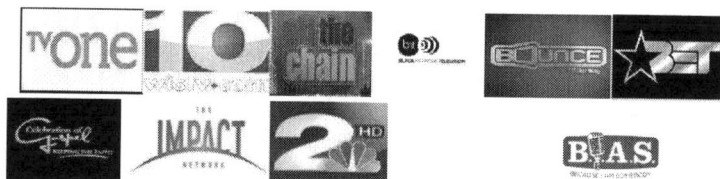

A MESSAGE FOR YOU:

I WANT TO TAKE THIS TIME TO THANK YOU
FOR SUPPORTING ME AND FOR ALWAYS
SHOWING UP TO CELEBRATE MY WINS WITH
ME AND FOR ENCOURAGING ME DURING
MY LOSES.

AS I TELL YOU ON A DAILY BASIS, YOU
HAVE EVERYTHING THAT YOU NEED ON
THE INSIDE OF YOU TO GET STARTED WITH
WHATEVER YOU DESIRE TO DO.

DON'T GET HUNG UP ON THE SMALL THINGS
LIKE WE OFTEN DO SOMETIMES. UNDERSTAND
THAT EVEN WHEN YOU FEEL AS IF YOU'RE
LOSING, REALITY IS: YOU'RE STILL WINNING!

WE ALL HAVE AN EXPECTED
END OF HAPPINESS, JOY AND FREEDOM.
WHAT'S EXPECTED OF US AND FOR US IS NOT
ALWAYS WHAT WE RECEIVE. THIS ISN'T
BECAUSE WE DON'T DESERVE IT. IT'S SIMPLY
BECAUSE WE'RE NOT EXPECTING IT FOR
OURSELVES.

TO:

FROM:

PUBLISHER: *Dr. Fred Jones*
Bestselling Author | Speaker | Coach
http://www.DrFredJones.Com (Want to write a book start here)

30836292R00057

Made in the USA
Middletown, DE
08 April 2016